MINDFULNESS

POEMS OF
LIFE AND LOVE

KATHRYN CAROLE ELLISON

Published by Lady Bug Books, an imprint of Brisance Books Group.
Lady Bug Press and the distinctive ladybug logo are registered trademarks of
Lady Bug Books, LLC.

Lady Bug Books
400 112th Avenue N.E.
Suite 230
Bellevue, WA 98004
www.GiftsOfLove.com

For information about custom editions, special sales and permissions, please email
Info@GiftsOfLove.com

Manufactured in the United States of America
ISBN: 978-1-944194-82-6

First Edition: October 2021

A NOTE FROM THE AUTHOR

The poems in this book were written over many years as gifts to my children. I began writing them in the 1970s, when they were reaching the age of reason. And, as I found myself in the position of becoming a single parent, I wanted to do something special to share with them — something that would become a tradition, a ritual they could count on.

And so the Advent Poems began — one day, decades ago — with a poem 'gifted' to them each day during the Advent period leading up to Christmas, December 1 to December 24. Forty some years later... my children still look forward each year to the poems that started a family tradition, that new generations have come to cherish.

It is my sincere hope that you will embrace and enjoy them, and share them with those you love.

Children of the Light was among the early poems I wrote, and is included in each of the *Poems of Life and Love* books in The Ellison Collection: *Heartstrings, Celebrations, Inspirations, Sanctuary, Awakenings, Sojourns, Milestones, Tapestry, Gratitude, Beginnings, Horizons, Moments, Possibilities, Mindfulness and Reflections*. After writing many hundreds of poems, it is still my favorite. The words came from my heart... and my soul... and flowed so effortlessly that it was written in a single sitting.
All I needed to do was capture the words on paper.

Light, to me, represented all that was good and pure and right with the world, and I believed then — as I do today — that those elements live in my children, and perhaps in all of us. We need only to dare.

– KCE

DEDICATION

To my parents: Herb and Bernice Haas

Mom, you were the poet who went before me...
unpublished, but appreciated nonetheless.

And Dad, you always believed in me,
no matter what direction my life took.
Thank you for your faith in me,
and for your unconditional love.

TABLE OF CONTENTS

LIFE'S JOYS

LIFE'S LESSONS

LIFE'S GIFTS

LIFE'S JOYS

MINDFULNESS

*...the psychological process of purposely bringing one's attention
to experiences occurring in the present moment, without judgment...*

Whatever the present moment contains,
Accept it as if you had chosen it.
Do not dwell in the past or dream of the future;
Only on the present moment can you commit.

The mind can be compared to water:
When it is turbulent it is difficult to see,
But when it is calm, everything becomes clear.
Mindfulness allows calmness and clarity.

Without judging, and by seeing everything for what it is,
You are free to be compassionate and kind.
To see yourself and others with kindness and compassion
Is a gift to the earth and to all of humankind.

Life is a dance, and mindfulness is witnessing it.
The goal is to see reality as it presents.
Mindfulness is a pause as you take it all in.
It's the space between stimulus and response.

PURITY

The love you get from God is pure,
And constant throughout your days.
No matter what, the love is there —
No strings, no demands, no delays.

Some people present erratic behavior
And are known for petty deeds.
This negativity abounds on earth
As people aspire to false needs.

Some will invert good to make negativity,
Saying it's God's Will, to get their way.
God has nothing to do with the harm
That rains down on earth day after day.

No, God presents good and God presents love
In its purest form there for the connection.
Choosing between light and darkness is
One aspect on your path to perfection.

LISTENING TO YOUR BODY

Your body is apt to be your autobiography –
So how on earth do you want it to read?
With bad habits and negative energy at every turn
Your body will respond badly – are we agreed?

But if you respect your body and its messages –
Listen closely, and acknowledge how you feel.
Do not follow the ideas of others; no, indeed.
Your body's messages will ultimately reveal
The truth as your body knows it, about how you are faring,
No matter what you've imagined that isn't real.
Be honest with yourself, and listen to your body.
Its messages are clear; you must listen with zeal.

Your body will never lie to you.
It's your mind that will try to play a trick.
You are worth the extra effort to take care of yourself,
So learn to listen and, about it, be quick!

The more you listen, the more you hear,
And the volume is variable, it would seem.
If you listen to your body when it whispers to you,
You won't have to some day hear it scream.

UNCONDITIONAL LOVE

Love is not determined by the one being loved,
But rather by the one who is choosing to love.
To love without need, without expectation
Of being loved in return is the way to love.

Once you understand love, you don't need a reward
For the kindness and compassion you give.
Do you need a reward for breathing the air?
No, air is necessary for you to live.

Love is not the opposite of power,
But instead the strongest power there is.
Unconditional love empowers the heart,
And fills it with self love... a promise.

Free of judgments and condemnation,
Unconditional love is desirable.
This love does not support, or be part of,
Another's behavior that is less than admirable.

When you love unconditionally you must give up
Your judgments of another's agitation.
You can then go inside and ask yourself
What to say and do in your conversation.

The answer will come from a platform of love,
Not of anger, resentment, guilt or judgment.
Your relationships with others will be more calm.
Your life will be filled with more enjoyment.

WORSHIP

The art of worship is an inner adventure,
Between you and your God, one on one.
Outer symbols can create mood and environment,
But it's personal when all is said and done.

Worship is meditation and prayer for expressing
The soul's innermost desire.
It's envisioning all that is heroic and good.
It's lifting your spirits higher.

It's cleansing your minds of fear and worry
So love can fill that space
With goodness, kindness, and blessings to bring
Big smiles upon your face.

Worship is counting your blessings... being thankful
For the power to grow and share
The love with others which moves us all forward
To the oneness which is so rare.

INTEGRITY

The magic keys to living your life with integrity
Are simple to say, but perhaps more difficult to do.
There are only three, and when first you hear them spoken
They sound simple enough, but the doing is left to you.

Have The Courage To Say No is the first of the three.
Next, **Have The Courage To Face The Truth** every day.
Finally, **Do The Right Thing**, because it's the right thing to do,
Whether anyone knows it or not... without delay.

Without integrity, friends, you have nothing at all.
There is not enough money anywhere in the world to buy it.
If you are not a moral and ethical person
You really have nothing at all, not one whit!

Integrity alone will not always make you a leader
But without integrity your leadership will fail miserably.
A true test of integrity is your refusal to be compromised.
You will do the right thing, have no guilt, and live peaceably.

LOAFING

He who finds time to loaf is a wise man, it's said.
You loaf and invite your soul,
Drifting and dreaming and opening yourself
To the inflow of peace. That's a goal!

Loafing is easing the pounding of your heart
By quieting your mind in your reverie.
It's relaxing the tension in your body with the music
Of the singing streams in your memory.

It's reminding yourself of the Hare and the Tortoise.
There's more to life than increasing its speed.
Loafing is sniffing a flower or chatting with a friend;
Petting a dog or planting a seed.

Loafing is using your hands to paint a picture
When that's not what you do for pay.
It's experiencing the adventure of changing your pace
From what you do every day.

Loaf with one eye open to catch flashes of light
That illuminate your mind with sought answers.
Let God's wisdom flow over and around.
Be known as one of life's romancers.

The art of loafing can add dimension and scope
To your life if you let yourself relax.
Changing your perspective and renewing your spirit,
Loafing allows you to live life to the "max."

SPIRITUAL AWARENESS

The purpose here is to praise spiritual awareness.
There is a way of knowing that is higher than reason,
And there is a Self that is greater than your ego.

When you are working with anyone else
The work must always include spiritual awareness...
To touch the existential anxiety of our times.

When awe is lacking, the awful remains unspoken,
Leaving a diffuse malaise in its wake.
There is no meaning or depth to your life.

It is wise to model spiritual behavior in your life,
So to live in harmony with spiritual value.
You demonstrate the unity of all creation.

IT'S OKAY TO SAY NO

Say yes to life; say yes to love;
Say yes to whatever you want.
But know that you have the right to say 'no'
When you think it is important.

It's said that saying no can be
The ultimate in self care.
Be strong in knowing that **you** choose
With whom and what you share.

No and Yes are just mere parts
Of the same continuum.
They're simply choices that **you** make;
It's okay to say 'No' with aplomb.

LOOK INSIDE

There are times when what the other fellows do
Is hard for even me to tolerate.
(I cannot think of many others who
Can patiently allow the other's state;
Can boast possession of so fine a trait.)
But sometimes when I'm pushed beyond the line
My patience for the antics withers on the vine.

The prize to me when I am in this mode?
Discomfort and a sense there's something wrong!
My own development is slightly bowed;
My heart sings a minutely off-key song.
My sense of self is not so very strong.
Since I can see the other fellow's flaws,
That they might also be within me – gives me pause.

It's this suspicion which can be an aid
To find what's troubling me about his deed.
And then a self-appraisal can be made...
To follow that, a plan that I can heed,
So by that healing I can then be freed.
It's through the loss of patience I can learn
To look inside, and watch my life make a turn.

SELF-AWARENESS

You have always been what you are. That's not new.
But knowing it, and acting accordingly? Whew!!!
That's the goal you must have, and not very much more...
To cut through those "acts," and get to the core.

No matter whom you love, or where you reside,
At your core you are always you. You can't hide!
Your visions will become clear; just look into your heart.
You will find you belong to yourself. That's a start!

Listen to the teachings your blood whispers to you.
In silence your own answers will filter through.
Do not do anything that is outside of your truth.
You will feel it when you do. You become your own sleuth.

Living a lie will reduce you to one.
Be true to yourself, and when the day is done,
You've kept yourself in sight. The world becomes your mirror;
And you step forward, no longer in fear.

Once yourself is known to you, you will learn
To take care of yourself. You are your first concern.
Self-knowledge is the basis for all knowledge. See?
As Lao Tze once said, 'The way to do is to be.'

STAYING IN TOUCH

It is said that in the final weeks of one's life
That love and relationships are the things that matter most.
Some people get too busy during their lives
For time with good friends; and golden friendships are lost.

It is common for people in a busy lifestyle
To let friendships slip, the togetherness to suspend.
But be careful when moving on in life
That the ones you lose are not true friends.

Taking care of business and getting affairs in order
Are important for one's peace of mind;
But money and status aren't important in the end.
Love and relationships take precedence, you will find.

Mystery

Some mysteries can be solved by conscious thought;
Examples are given on TV, are they not?
A murderer or robber is usually taken
Just before the final ad for Armour Bacon.

Yet, some mysteries exist that are not to be explained.
In matters such as these, our minds are restrained.

The mystery of self is not to be revealed
By examining each part of you that is concealed.
The more you try to fathom what's inside
The further out-of-reach the clues reside.

The need to know it all must surely be sustained
By some primordial gene that is pre-ingrained.

The resistance of the self to be analyzed
Is key to the way that the self is scrutinized.
You do not solve the mystery, but you live it.
Not "knowing;" instead "living" to your limit.

YOURSELF

Descartes said, "I think, therefore I am."
But does saying and thinking make it so?
Perhaps it does, but after you ponder,
Move on. There's more to the show!

Like dew that vanishes, or like a phantom
That disappears before your eyes,
Is how you should think about yourself
If you're on the path to be wise.

The light cast by a flash of lightning –
An instant, and then it is gone –
Is how you should perceive your being.
It's not to be dwelled upon.

Because it's when your thoughts disappear
That Zen begins to be.
Zen means doing ordinary things,
Willingly and cheerfully.

LIFE'S LESSONS

HEAR YOUR INNER VOICE

If each step you take feels good to you,
You must be headed in the right direction.
When your inner voice agrees with what you're doing,
You know you've made the right selection.

Measure your progress against an inner compass,
Using feelings and self-knowledge as your guide.
Your comfort level is your voice of reason
As your life's travels take you on your ride.

The inner voice sometimes is hard to hear
Because of the noise around you every day,
But listen closely to its vital message.
It tells you truths you must obey.

You softly hear the inner voice explain
That happiness can be as simple a thing
As having something to look forward to each day;
That now's the time to have fun. Happy Living!

CONSULT YOURSELF

Where your life is concerned, you are the pro.
You know yourself better than others do.
In order to live at your own tempo,
The burden of decision rests solely on you.

Sometimes it's hard to remember this teaching,
Especially when others so willingly give
Opinions expressed with a barrage of preaching.
Your outcome is one with which you must live.

In order to consult well, you must trust
That secret place you have inside;
And know that all has been discussed
With One in whom you can confide.

God lives in you, right at your core.
He celebrates and suffers full.
You have His wisdom, you don't need more.
The answers are within, so pull!

SPEAK ONLY WITH GOOD PURPOSE

Much attention is given to the moral importance
Of your acts and deeds, and rightly so, I am sure.
But in seeking the higher life you must consider
The moral power of the words that you utter!

One of the clearer marks of the moral life
Is right speech in your daily use.
Thinking before speaking is one of the ways
To make sure you're speaking with good purpose.

Glib talk disrespects others; breezy, self–disclosure, yourself.
The random dump of the content of one's mind
Is like a vehicle wildly lurching out of control
And destined for destruction of some kind.

Speech itself is neither good nor evil,
But it is used carelessly in everyday interaction.
It is unbecoming to be a chatterbox.
Prattle defeats your higher purpose. It is a distraction.

SELF-CONFIDENCE

An important key to success is self-confidence,
And the key to self-confidence is preparation.
You're the only person on earth who can use your ability,
So move forward, step by step, with inspiration.

Nothing builds self-esteem better than accomplishment.
Do the things you fear and build on your success.
If you've done a little thing well, you can do a bigger one well, too.
Soon your accomplishments are seemingly effortless.

Self-confidence is the most attractive quality you can have,
And you must see it in yourself in order for others to see it.
Face your fear; gain strength and confidence in the doing.
You can listen to others' stories, but unfold your own myth.

Don't surround yourself with people who are not aware
Of the greatness that you are, and the skills you own.
Fall in love with yourself, and accomplish your own goals.
The universe will affirm your worth. This fact is well known.

IMPERMANENCE

Every change is a challenge to become who you are,
And hopefully, you will always be changing.
When one stage of life gives way to another
Your habits will need rearranging.
How you spiritually navigate these important transitions
Will determine whether joy or despair is ranging.

There is never a permanent positive change.
Everything everywhere is impermanent.
Every beginning has an end; everything born will die.
(Moves so fast we're left in bewilderment)
We're not stagnant beings. Transience is a given.
Relax, live in the moment. Take enjoyment.

No man ever steps in the same river twice.
It's not the same river, keeps on flowing.
And it's not the same man, for between the steps
Man is changing, the winds are blowing.
The only way to make sense of the changes
Is to move with them, join the dance, go on growing.

If you decide to avoid change at all costs,
Be prepared for a life-changing shock!
Change will eventually find you in your hiding,
And it probably won't even knock.
Robert Frost summed up all he learned about life
In three words: "It goes on." (Tick Tock)

LIVE IN A LARGE MORAL HOUSE

A large house usually has many rooms;
Each one is there for a special reason:
One for cooking and eating and one for sleep,
And maybe one just for that special season.

Imagine our world as a house with many rooms,
And each room is filled with a different nation.
If the house could run smoothly, imagine the shock!
It would be something of a major sensation.

We all live together in a large moral house
Though we may not drink from the same fountain of belief.
The problems we face are the same in every room;
Common human problems that bring people grief.

Talking to each other to share the woes
Of dealing with life and the challenges to be met
Is a way to bring our nations together
And find better ways to "sing a duet."

Think about the ways your own world has improved
With knowing someone from a different nation.
What have you learned? What insights have you gained
By finding the words and their translation?

CENTERING

Rumi asks a question most direct
Regarding your travel plans, and the timing:
"And you? When will you begin... the journey...
That long journey into yourself?" (The incredible climb.)

Centering can be a lifelong struggle,
Especially if you let your emotions rule.
Quiet your emotions and enjoy the peace.
(You did not learn these things in school.)

Kareem Abdul Jabbar (that tall man)
Likened centering to the game of basketball.
He said, "Don't forget... you play with your soul
As well as with your body." (He made the call.)

Perhaps centering is simply getting the two in tandem —
The physical and the spiritual, side by side —
Pulling together, sharing the journey,
In balance with each other... enjoying the ride.

When centered, you are able to simply observe
And not be tossed this way or that.
When calmness prevails, when you are centered,
Your decisions are no longer 'drawn from a hat.'

COMMITMENT

The quality of people's lives, I've been told,
Is in direct proportion to their commitment to excellence.
Their chosen field of endeavor doesn't matter.
Success is usually guaranteed, once they commence.

It was character that first got you out of bed,
And commitment that moved you into action.
Discipline enabled you to follow through,
And finish the job with satisfaction.

Commitment is an act, and not just a word.
You need discipline and hard work to get you there.
That's called follow–through – you roll up your sleeves,
And put your best foot forward, with care.

The only limit to your impact, my loves,
Is your imagination and commitment to your goal.
Without commitment there are only promises and hopes,
But no plans... so, make them. You are in control.

WISDOM

The race that some humans undertake
To gather the lion's share of knowledge
Sends some to study with gurus wise,
While others opt to attend a college.

Some say knowledge is learning something every day,
Something you didn't know before.
Perhaps that's correct, but who knows for sure?
After all, who is keeping score?

Learning is one thing; discernment is another,
And some information is pretty silly.
Pay attention to your lessons as you take them in;
Don't accept everything you hear, willy-nilly.

Knowledge alone, without wisdom to guide
Can clutter the mind, or didn't you know?
While knowledge is learning something every day,
True wisdom is every day letting go.

THROUGH GRATITUDE
TO SELF WORTH

To expand on the subject of self-worth –
Without it our perspectives are distorted.
We must respect and love ourselves first,
Then we're free to love others, it's reported.

Without the freedom of standing alone,
Another in a relationship becomes a crutch
Upon whom we must lean for all our support.
For either one, it's not fun... not much.

Some ways I have learned to build self-worth
I'll pass on to the two of you "tykes."
I'll keep a copy to refer back to if,
On a dark day, I forget, and fear strikes.

Yes, fear is the culprit... the opposite of love.
(We grew up thinking it was hate.)
Fear cripples and distorts and keeps us bound
To non-positive views of fate.

I clearly believe we create our own fate.
We alone can control our own life.
Keeping thoughts positive, then living by them,
Keeps our mental pictures free of strife.

Gratitude is an important requirement
To obtain a happy demeanor.
We often fail to forget what we have,
And our dispositions get meaner.

Be grateful for what you have, my dears.
Believe me, you're well endowed
With gifts that surpass your wildest of dreams...
All of which make me very proud.

VERITY

Truths appear to us, sometimes, out of the blue
When we're least expecting them to arrive.
They cause us to think about the things of importance
That let us know we are alive!

This truth came to me: "If you love someone
As they are, you're never disappointed."
Then, "If we try to make them what they're not
Our minds become disjointed."

And wishing things were different, when they can never be
Other than the way they are?
Be true to yourself, I guess I'm saying,
And you are sure to go far.

It's interesting, isn't it, and also ironic,
How it always comes back to say:
"To thine own self be true." The truth never changes.
It's a verity that is here to stay.

SURROUND YOURSELF WITH LOVE

At times the world seems filled with rude people
Who don't treat their fellow man well.
It's hard at times to be around those so artless.
In fact, it makes you want to yell,
"Get off my case, you ignorant fool!
You've no right to treat me like you do!"
Of course, others should not act so bad,
But they do, and control first begins with you.
Surround yourself with those who treat you well;
Who respect that you're a valid individual.
You'll find that you will grow into their view of you,
And the respect and treatment will be mutual.

CHILDREN OF THE LIGHT

There are those souls who bring the light,
Who spill it out for all to share.
And with a joy that does excite,
They show the world that they do care.
It is so very bright.

In this sharing, love does pervade
Into their lives and cycles round;
And as this light is outward played
The love is also inward bound.
It is an awesome trade.

You are a soul whose light is shared.
It comes from deep within your heart.
It's best because it is not spared,
Because it's total, not just part.
And I am glad you've dared.

WHETHER YOU KNOW IT OR NOT

You do not have to join a study group
Or lead one through all of its dealings
In order for your life to work for you,
Or to learn to be in charge of your feelings.

The continuum of life unfolds regardless
And conflicts will eventually get resolved.
Whether or not you can make things happen,
The cycles of life will gradually evolve.

Being aware of how things happen heightens
The power and effectiveness of behavior.
In every era and culture, people have honored
The ones who make things happen as superior.

HAPPINESS

A subject about which much has been written,
The pursuit of happiness can put you in a spin.
Strive for it, go in search of it, wait for it to happen –
Your happiness can come, but only from within.

Happiness is not something that is ready-made.
It comes only from your own actions – it's true.
It's dependent upon your own mental attitude.
It's not so hard, but the onus is on you.

Our Constitution gives us the right to pursue it.
There's no guarantee that happiness will come.
Any happiness you get... you've got to catch it yourself!
Waiting for it to happen can be wearisome.

The happiest people are those who are giving –
Rather than getting – in all likelihood.
Happiness is not a goal; it is merely a by-product
Of using the talents you are given to do good.

The choices you make will determine the degree
Of happiness or unhappiness in your daily lives.
Consequences will always follow your choices.
Use your talents for good and you will thrive.

MISTAKES... AND LESSONS LEARNED

Everyone makes mistakes,
Though we try to do our best.
The ancients would only say:
"Errare humanum est."*

But there are people in this world
Who would comment when we blunder,
Who let us know we goofed.
Here's a way to steal their thunder:
Acknowledge you've made a mistake.
(You're very human throughout.)
Smile, and politely say,
"Thanks for pointing that out."

Then use that information
To make changes and enhance
Your happiness and success.
It is a second chance.

* It is human to err.

LIFE'S GIFTS

HARMONY

Happiness occurs when what you think,
What you say, and what you do are in harmony.
You know how you feel when one part is missing.
It take all three parts to live doubt-free.
Always aim at harmony of thought, word and deed.
Happiness will follow. It is a guarantee.

Happiness is not a matter of intensity,
But of balance, order, harmony and rhythm.
No matter how excited you can get about something,
The intensity does not bring harmony... or even wisdom.
The universe is not required to bring harmony.
It's up to you. You're in charge of the outcome.

What is happiness but the simple harmony between
A person and the life which he or she leads?
When that balance or that harmony goes away,
Happiness disappears. Are we agreed?
Be in harmony with yourself and your life will run smoothly,
For with harmony in your life you can proceed.

FAITH

Optimism is the faith that leads to achievement.
Nothing can be done without confidence and hope.
And faith is a passionate intuition you possess.
Against all odds and setbacks you will cope.
Faith will give you an inner strength, a confidence...
A sense of balance and ability to keep things in scope.

Faith is a knowledge within your heart
That reaches beyond any limits of evidence.
It is reason grown courageous; a state of trust.
And the principal part of faith is patience.
With faith you can trust without reservation.
Believe in yourself; you'll move forth with confidence.

EXERCISE

You will never get the ass you want
But continuing to sit on it, not moving.
Exercise is your choice to start on the path
To gain the look you're approving.

A one-hour workout is just four percent
Of your entire twenty-four hour day.
What you can accomplish in an hour of exercise
Will increase your good health along the way.

You'll notice that with exercise your energy level
Increases, and you feel stronger, by far...
Not only stronger, but clearer in mind!
Make exercise a habit... it improves your vascular!

Life can be compared to a ten-speed bike –
Most of us have gears we never use.
You get what you work for! That's the truth!
Do the work; don't make the excuse.

And don't dig your grave with your own knife and fork!
Pay attention to your diet – stay engrossed.
Discipline is choosing between what you want now,
And what you really want most!

BALANCE

The Moody Blues an album did
On the very subject at hand.
"A Question Of Balance" they named the work,
And they sang to beat the band.

The subject has a history from the beginning of time.
Of course, you know that to be true.
The greatest philosophers of all times
Have given "Balance" a moment or two.

The concept is simple, keep all three equal –
Physical, mental and spiritual ways.
But "simple" does not mean easy, as you know;
You work to maintain balance all of your days.

My advice to you, for what it is worth,
Is to listen to your voices equally.
Your body, your head and your heart all talk.
Listen to them, and then you can see
Which way to go, what paths to take;
(I'm writing to myself, as well)
Which moves to move, which friends to meet...
That's as much on the subject that I can tell.

I know it to be true. On every level
I'm as sure of it as I've ever been sure.
Just ask, and your three "friends" will kick in,
To keep your paths noble and pure.

DREAMS ARE FREE

Coming true is not the only purpose of a dream,
Because dreams are based on the premise, "What if?"
Let your imagination run wild and visualize
All that you want to have in your life.

The most important purpose of a dream
Is to get in touch with the place dreams originate;
And where passion and happiness come from, as well.
Then look to see how reality and dreams relate.

You can make your dreams work and produce for you...
What comes into your mind can pay a dividend.
Your imagination will show you the path to take
To bring your dream to reality; your fears you'll transcend.

JUDGMENT

Your soul cannot be judged by anyone
Living today (or not) on this planet.
Nobody has dominion over your spirit.
This fact is one you ought not forget.

Which means, of course, you cannot judge
Another's soul in return.
It's possible to judge their acts, of course,
As they judge yours — no concern.

We are all subject to social law —
It's how we learn to get along —
But only God can judge our souls.
If we try it, we're in the wrong.

OBSERVATION

People's minds are changed, not by argument,
But through their own observations.
All the words, the energy, the stress of debate
Are worthless against their interpretations.

Nothing has such power to broaden the mind
As the ability to investigate
All that comes under one's observation in life.
On that you must concentrate.

The prime educators, as described by Alcott,*
Are not what one might think.
"Observation more than books, and experience more than persons;"
From this well of knowledge you must drink.

For acquiring great knowledge it's necessary to study;
To acquire wisdom you must observe.
Accuracy of observation correlates to accuracy of thinking.
They go hand in hand, the rewards you deserve.

As a little side joke, Will Rogers once stated:
"There are three kinds of men in this world (not twelve):
One learns by reading, a few by observation.
The rest have to pee on the electric fence for themselves."

*Amos Bronson Alcott

TRUST IN YOURSELF

If you mistrusted your friends like you
mistrust your own being,
They'd drop you like a hot potato, and
run away, fleeing.
"Trust in yourself" is my advice for
you this day;
And trust in your perceptions
as you go along your way.

They are, without a doubt, more fitting
to your needs
Than any others' perceptions or their
individual deeds.
You have to know that you are the captain
of your ship;
You have what it takes for your
own championship.

VALUE JUDGMENTS

Value judgments can be a mistake...
They can close your mind to learning.
Should you decide that big things are better,
Then small things you're automatically spurning.

In the landscape of Spring, there's no "better" or "worse."
Flowering branches grow naturally, short and long.
Beauty cannot be limited in its scope;
Indeed, all forms of it belong.

Little trees and big trees have their unique uses.
Short is not better than tall.
The little things in life are as interesting as the big.
There is room in this world for all.

As you live throughout your days on this earth,
Live them with good intent.
Don't limit yourself by narrowing your scope,
And your life will be magnificent.

RENEWAL

As each year rolls around to your birthday,
It's a good time to do an inventory
So you can begin, renewed and free
From repeating the same old story.

Looking to the past gives a guide to your future.
It's a good time to sort out the negative;
To toss those old resentments and fears,
And give yourself a new directive:
A time to examine the things left undone
And to do something about them now...
To make that visit or finish that task...
To examine your life and re-avow.

Renewal allows you to dust off your dreams;
To shine up your ideals once again...
To see where you are and where you want to go,
And to go forward with a grin.

It's a good time to reread those precious old books
And letters that have brought so much pleasure;
A time to give thanks for all that you are
And all that you have to treasure.

It's a time to resolve to add life to your years,
A time of rededication
To things that endure: The great use of life
Is spent on eternal creation.

PERCEPTION

LOOK AGAIN:
If at first you don't like what you see –
If you think you've really lost your key –
RETHINK IT:
If you feel afraid or if you're in pain –
If you're suffering from a frazzled brain –
OPEN YOUR EYES:
Your lives depend entirely on perception.
Your views are the fruit of your conception.
CHANGE YOUR THOUGHT PATTERNS
You have a choice of things to think about.
You can forget the past and lose the doubt.
SEE JOY IN ALL THINGS:
Use the past to move from 'there' to 'here.'
Choose to rebuild traits you can revere.
THINK LOVING THOUGHTS:
Hold loving thoughts forever in your mind,
And positive perceptions will follow close behind.

A CLOSING THOUGHT

Poetry

It's the revelation
Of a sensation
That the poet
(Wouldn't you know it)
Believes to be
Felt only interiorly
And personal to
The writer who
... **writes it.**

It's the interpretation
Of a sensation
That was fueled by
A poet's sigh
And believed to be
Shared mutually
And personal to
The lucky one who
... **reads it.**

ABOUT THE AUTHOR

Kathryn Carole Ellison is a former newspaper columnist
and journalist and, of course, a poet.

She lives near her children and stepchildren and their families in the
Pacific Northwest, and spends winters in the sunshine of Arizona.

You might find her on the golf course with friends, river rafting, traveling
the world, writing poems... or enjoying the Opera and the Symphony.

LATE BLOOMER

Our culture honors youth with all
It's unbridled effervescence.
We older ones sit back and nod
As if in acquiescence.

And when our confidence really gels
In early convalescence...
"We can't be getting old!" we cry,
"We're still struggling with adolescence!"

Acknowledgments

I have many people to thank...

First of all, my amazing children—Jon and Nicole LaFollette—for inspiring the writing of these poems in the first place. And for encouraging me to continue my writing, even though their wisdom and compassion surpass mine... and to my dear daughter-in-law and friend, Eva LaFollette, whose encouragement and interest are so appreciated.

My wonderful stepchildren, Debbie and John Bacon, Jeff and Sandy Ellison, and Tom and Sue Ellison who, with their children and grandchildren, continue to be a major part of my life; and are loved deeply by me. These poems are for you, too.

My good friends who have received a poem or two of mine in their Christmas cards these many years, for complimenting me on the messages in my poems. Your encouragement kept me writing and gave me the courage to publish.

To Kim Kiyosaki who introduced me to the right person to get the publishing process under way... Mona Gambetta with Brisance Books Group. I marvel at her experience and know-how to make these books happen.

To Amy Anderson, Sonya Kopetz, Kerri Kazarba Schneider, and Ingrid Pape-Sheldon, my very creative public relations team of experts, who have carried my story to the world.

And finally, to John B. Laughlin, a fellow traveler in life, who encourages me every day in the writing and publishing process. John, I love having you in my cheering section.

BOOKS OF LOVE
by Kathryn Carole Ellison